SCORCHED BY THE SUN

BOOKS IN ENGLISH BY MOSHE DOR:

The Fullness Thereof, 2002 (chapbook)
Khamsin: Memoirs and Poetry by a Native Israeli, 1994
Crossing the River, 1989
Maps of Time, 1978

SCORCHED BY THE SUN

poems by Moshe Dor
translated from the Hebrew by
Barbara Goldberg and Moshe Dor

INTERNATIONAL EDITIONS

THE WORD WORKS
WASHINGTON, D.C.

FIRST EDITION FIRST PRINTING
Scorched by the Sun
Copyright © 2012 by Moshe Dor

Reproduction of any part of this book in any form or by any means, electronic or mechanical, including photocopying, must be with permission in writing from the publisher. Address inquiries to:

The WORD WORKS
PO Box 42164
Washington, DC 20015

wordworksbooks.org
editor@wordworksbooks.org

Cover art: *Red Sun*, by Mordecai Ardon. Israel Museum, permanent exhibition at the National and University Library in Givat Ram, near the Ardon Windows

Translator's photo: Jill Finsen

Book design, typography: Janice Olson

Library of Congress Control Number: 2011938038
International Standard Book Number: 978-0-915380-83-1

Acknowledgments

Thanks to the following publications where these poems first appeared:

Agni: "Coffee Thoughts"

American Poetry Review: "There Are Just Wars"

Counterfeits: Two Lines: World Literature in Translation (Rosanna Warren, ed.), California Center for the Art of Translation: "At the End"

Fine Madness: "A Military Correspondent Remembers"

Harvard Review: "Silence of the Builder"

Modern Poetry in Translation: "By the Rivers of Babylon"

Pale House: "Echo," "Linguistics"

Salmagundi: "In Praise of Hate"

The Fullness Thereof (chapbook, Dryad Press, 2002): "Destroyer in Eden," "Earthquake," "Silence of the Builder," "Tongues," "Your Window"

Tikkun: "Silence"

Our thanks to the Institute for the Translation of Hebrew Literature (NPO), the MacDowell Colony and the Maryland State Arts Council for their kind assistance in making this translation possible.

CONTENTS

    Translator's Preface   9

    Poppy   13

I. THERE ARE WARS

    Smells   17
    Wiping the Plate Clean   18
    Earthly Thoughts on Hazohar Street at the Threshold of the Millennium   19
    Happiness   20
    Redbud in Dalia   21
    Tombstone   22
    Linguistics   23
    Siege   24
    Shelter   25
    There Are Just Wars   26
    Fantasies   27
    The Coastal Road, Before Dawn   28
    A Military Correspondent Remembers   29
    Silence   30
    Sequel   31
    Echo   32
    Lately Dead People   33
    Siren   34

II. OASIS

    You Didn't Ask   37
    Topography   38
    Fingers   39
    Direction   40

At the Acupuncturist's Waiting Room	41
Tongues	42
Your Window	43
Innocence	44
Citronella	45
Lacework	46
Destroyer in Eden	47
Borrowed Time	48
Earthquake	49
Asteroid	50
Hush	51
Noon, on Fairfax Road	52
Extremities	53
Houses	54
By the Rivers of Babylon	55
At the End	56

III. KNIFE IN THE RIBS

Web	59
Loss	60
Sibboleth	61
Earth	62
Silence of the Builder	63
Cassandras	64
Megiddo	65
Cage	66
Fall	67
Nantucket	68
Windfall	69
Insomnia	70
I Dreamed of a General	71
Heaviness	72

Fall Back	73
If It Were Fall	74
Holy City	75
I Ran	76
Abraham	77
Calendar	79
Coffee Thoughts	80

IV. THE HEART'S FIELD OF STUBBLE

Vagaries of Time	83
In Praise of Hate	84
In My Dream My Life	85
It's Easier to Lament	86
Coming Back	87
Motherland	88
Distance	89
Times	90
Ninth Month	91
Long Distance	92
And They Merit Glory	93
Poems from the Rented House	94
Do You Remember	99
Divisions	100
Just in Spite	101
Joy	102
Aroma	103
Request	104
About the Author	106
About the Translator	107
About The Word Works	108
Word Works Books	109

TRANSLATOR'S PREFACE

THE *SABRA* IS A TENACIOUS, THORNY DESERT PLANT. Carefully peel off its thick hide and you'll find the fruit inside deliciously sweet. This cactus variety is also known as the prickly pear.

Sabra is also a nickname for a native-born Israeli, suggesting that even though Israeli sabras are rough and masculine on the outside, they are delicate and sensitive on the inside.

Moshe Dor is a sabra—Hebrew is his mother tongue and Israel is his motherland. Born in Tel Aviv in 1932, he has a sabra's love for the Land of Israel. He is acutely aware that he dwells among historical landscapes. The rose of Sharon and the lilies of that valley bloom, after all, on Tel Aviv's doorstep. The tamarisks under which the patriarch Abraham sat are within walking distance of Ben Gurion University in the Negev.

Dor's poems are stamped with the consciousness of past-as-present. Current events unfold in biblical landscapes. Megiddo, the Hebrew word for Armageddon, is also an Israeli kibbutz close to where a bus was blown up by a Palestinian suicide bomber. Megiddo is no mere geographic reference, but literally and metaphorically a place of doom.

To see Tel Aviv today, it's hard to believe the city is built on sand. In 1932, it was a little town with coarse *zifzif* sand rustling under one's bare toes. Sand dunes ran all the way down to the sea. Camel caravans passed, bells clanging on their swaying necks. Wild vines clothed the hills.

This is the landscape of Dor's youth, the motherland he clings to and yearns for. It will not let him go, even when, years later, he stands on the threshold of a house in Maryland: "the knife of your memory/ lodges in my ribs, burning." ("If It Were Fall")

But Dor has another love—the love of a man for a woman. He brings to both the same passion. He is at home in his motherland and also with his woman, but always in exile from one or the other. Only in his imagination can these two loves become one. "My motherland is your bodyland," he writes in "Topography." The hills and plains of the Israeli landscape are likened to the hills and plains of a woman's body:

> My motherland is
> your bodyland:
> your breasts—the hills
> of Jerusalem,
> your belly—the coastal plain,
> and between your thighs sometimes
> the saltiness of the Dead Sea
> and sometimes
> the sweet Kinneret.

Integration of woman into country and country into woman is a continuing struggle. And from this struggle poems emerge that express the freshness of love, its joys, fears, its little daily delights. Here is Dor in the Hatikva section of Tel Aviv, "Wiping the Plate Clean" of hummus:

> Levy Yitzhak, Elisheva and I are wiping
> hummus off our plates in Hatikva quarter,
> rolling memories about like falafel.
> Sabbath belongs to God
> and hummus to Man.....

Here he is drinking strong coffee in the afterlife, sharing gossip with friends. And here he is in "Fingers" with the woman he loves, holding hands—a small gesture replete with intimacy:

> When you entwine your fingers in mine
> I know it was worthwhile to take
> my old knapsack, pack it with the motherland's image
> and other basic necessities and set forth, middle-aged
> and scarred by my past...

Just as love for both motherland and woman is pure and innocent, so is hate. "Heaviness" expresses hatred towards both woman and country: "Everything/ is heavy on me, and in me, my country/ is heavy and my misfortune/ is heavy and my hate/ for you is heavy..."

Another element of Dor's poetry is *hamatzav*—the "situation." Hamatzav is a Hebrew expression every Israeli understands. Cab drivers, grocers, professors, family and friends, after the obligatory, "How goes?" will ask, "So. What do you think about hamatzav?" And they will give you—uninvited—an earful of their views. The conflict, elections, the latest scandal, Israel is always in the midst of a "situation." It is an ever-present fact of Israeli life, the backdrop against which all emotions and endeavors are projected, the convoluted, crooked, tortured and tortuous human condition with its special Israeli twist. It means always living under the gun. It means hope and terror living side by side, the agony of war and the craving for peace inextricably intertwined.

Dor is well acquainted with the agony of war. In pre-State Israel, while still in high school, he joined the Hagana underground. Since its inception in 1948, Israel has fought many wars. In the army as a military correspondent. Dor wrote:

> In that war there was no Central Front
> but I keep brooding on the central
> point to a story about the harsh sound
> scrapers make when peeling charred flesh
> off the inner seams of a burnt-out tank.

Dor's hope is that Jew and Arab can reconcile, as did Jacob and Esau, the twin sons of Isaac and Rebecca. Isaac is the forebear of the Israelites. Isaac's half brother Ishmael is considered to be the Father of the Arabs.

This is why in "Linguistics" Dor writes: "Hebrew and Arabic are blood/relatives, perhaps even cousins..." The two languages are related, with the words for "salt" and "honey" remarkably similar.

Dor's poems are rich in allusions to the Hebrew Bible. They also revel in puns and word play. Some resonances of the original may be lost on English-speaking readers. But no matter the language, there is always something "lost" in translation.

They say that translation is like kissing a bride through a veil. They also say that if the bride (the translation) is beautiful, she is not faithful (doesn't stick to the literal), and if she is faithful, she is not beautiful. Are beauty and fidelity really mutually exclusive? The challenge for the translator is to preserve the poem's underlying core, to convey the freshness, spirit and musicality of the original, to make the poem "sing."

Dor is a lyric poet par excellence—all his poems are love poems. Even when they express hate. He is also a great lyricist. His *erev shel shoshanim (Evening of Roses)* is a favorite wedding song for brides all over the globe. Indeed, Dor's poems embrace the whole spectrum of human emotion, by turns cheerful and tragic, delicate and aggressive, ecstatic and tormented. You can find it all here.

Barbara Goldberg
Chevy Chase, Maryland

POPPY

*In the heart's field of stubble
blooms a lone poppy. Look at it.
Carve its valor on memory's slate:
upright, solitary, red, despite not knowing
if, or when, it will perish from the world
of flora. Indeed, this is my Land
of Israel, staunch in the face of reality,
refusing to become a work of art: a single
poppy in the heart's field of stubble.*

THERE ARE WARS

SMELLS

Spring hasn't arrived, but in my dream my nostrils fill
with your smell, lost motherland, the smell of eucalypti
on the banks of the Yarkon on a sunny day,

the smell of oil from gas stations along the coastal plain,
falafel browning in frying pans, pine resin wafting
down from the hills, wine foaming in the presses...

I inhale avidly, my eyes smarting. Capricious fate
has overturned all maps. I awake befuddled,
not knowing where I am, groping for a warm

body to define the boundaries of my life. Spring
hasn't arrived, but in my dream my nostrils fill
with your smell, and all seasons bloom in my heart.

WIPING THE PLATE CLEAN

Levy Yitzhak, Elisheva and I are wiping
hummus off our plates in Hatikva quarter,
rolling memories about like falafel.
Sabbath belongs to God
and hummus to Man.

And where are Ronny and Rafi?
They are cracking sunflower seeds
while watching a historic soccer match
that will decide which team advances
to the finals, applauding and cursing
as needs be. And it's a spring day,
the margosa trees are blooming, violet
as in childhood, the bougainvillea flaming
on the fences and a light breeze from the sea
refreshing exhausted souls, and suddenly
there's no nuclear threat, no terror, no
famine, no pestilence.

And you, my darling, where are you?
Beyond seas and mountains of darkness you waver
between debating the importance of Judaic traditions
and your appointment at the hair dresser's, back
and forth, getting more lost by the minute.

Final whistle. The crowd goes wild, the winning
team's fans dancing in the field under the generous
sun, Ronny wiping a tear, Rafi speechless, and in
Hatikva quarter, Levy Yitzhak, Elisheva and I
sweeten the bitter Turkish coffee with gossip, torn
between eating baklava—on the house—now
or later, feeling new hope flooding in,
filling the chambers of our hearts.

EARTHLY THOUGHTS ON HAZOHAR STREET
AT THE THRESHHOLD OF THE MILLENNIUM

Do you still feel history walks beside you
on your way
to the grocery store?

Stretch your hand to the ficus
still moist from morning rain, pluck
a dark green leaf, roll it till your fingers
become sticky, earthly, exactly
how fingers are meant to feel.

That way the motherland of hunger
and satiation, heat and cold, will come
back to you. The grass sprouting
through cracks in the sidewalks, the spring
sky, bereft of angels, gilding the cleavage
of the beautiful woman you love.

When you return with a loaf of bread
under your arm, you will have shed
history, but be filled with sunshine
and shade and the scent of freshly
baked bread, the way a person should be
walking to the grocery store and coming back.

Hazohar: Hebrew for the splendor or radiance. The Book of Zohar is considered the most important work of Kabbalah (Jewish mysticism).

HAPPINESS

The Negev *agama* sips
the sun in minute, rhythmic mouthfuls.
Its throat is almost transparent.
It is half light itself.

These languid days of summer
drowse on a thicket of olive trees,
each with a triple trunk: past,
present, future.

If you now draw
your face close to mine
it could be happiness.

Agama: lizard.

REDBUD IN DALIA

The redbud in Dalia blooms
like my lost, rosy-fingered
love. From where I stand
the hills of Ephraim arch
like her young, firm breasts
and a stubborn woodpecker
hammers at the heart
of a world that remains
bright as a diamond
and as impenetrable.

TOMBSTONE

Carved on David Ben Gurion's tombstone
at Sdeh Boker are the dates of his birth,
his death, and the year of his *aliyah*—

1906—as if his real life began
when he emigrated here and everything
before then was of little import.

On a day of parched lips, how beautiful
that pepper tree planted by the old man's
own hands by the cottage he lived in
more than 53 years ago: now it's a tree
casting a glorious shade; before
there was nothing.

The wilderness is splendid with its lofty
pillars, awe-inspiring canyons, and the savage
colors at dusk are breathtaking, but
Hebrew arms confirm that water equals life.

Blessed be thou breeze that cools
my feverish brow, dries the sweat
salting my back, shades the plot where I
find shelter from the desert sun's wrath.

Nabateans, Romans, Arabs, Turks
and British lived here and moved on
but tonight poetry will be recited,
the stars so close you could pluck them
from the sky but you won't because
they are protected flowers.

David Ben Gurion, nicknamed "The Old Man," is the Founding Father of Israel and its first Prime Minister. He joined kibbutz Sdeh Boker in the Negev in the early 1950s and lived there until his death in 1973. His burial place and the cottage where he lived with his wife are a national site. Sdeh Boker is also famous for its annual Poetry Festival. *Aliyah* in Hebrew means immigration to the Land of Israel.

LINGUISTICS

And he beat down the city and sowed it with salt.
                                        Judges, ch. 9, v. 45

*Mine eyes have been enlightened because I tasted
a little of this honey.*
                                        Samuel I, ch. 14, v. 29

Hebrew and Arabic are blood relatives—
perhaps even cousins. Salt in Hebrew
is *melakh,* in Arabic, *milkh.* Honey
in Hebrew is *dvash,* in Arabic, *dibsh.*
Whether salt or honey will prevail has nothing
to do with linguistics. The dark heart
shall decide: either the salty desolation
wreaked by Abimelech, or Jonathan's honeycomb.

SIEGE

> *When thou shalt besiege a city a long time, in making war against it to take it, thou shalt not destroy the trees thereof by forcing an ax against them: for thou mayest eat of them, and thou shalt not cut them down for man is the tree of the field.*
> Deuteronomy, ch. 20, v. 19

It's not true that the hand of he who cuts down
an olive tree trembles when lifting the ax.

Let's dispense with symbols. This
is not literature. This is life diminishing
with every thud of an ax, every screech
of a chainsaw, but it does not cry out
because it doesn't have a voice.

Every day faces blush anew, not
from shame, but from blood spilling
on both sides of the invisible border,
staining olive leaves and the flesh
of man because he is
the tree of the field.

And if among the trampled branches a bird
drops dead in the night, it is not
from flying over the land in search
of an olive leaf, but from West Nile
fever, known also for killing humans.

SHELTER

We cleaned out the bomb shelter,
a municipal edict too stringent
to ignore. We worked diligently:
an iron bedstead with protruding springs,
broken utensils, a shard of mirror,
a plastic container whose contents
evaporated a long time ago, the junk
of life, all collected and dumped.

Now that the shelter has been restored
to its original condition, we are filled
with a sense of our own virtue, cleansed
of sloth and regret. Now we can wait
for evil from any direction. Only
our image reflected in that sliver
of mirror is slightly blurred, perhaps
because we have let down our guard.
How quickly dust accumulates on the glass.

THERE ARE JUST WARS

and there are wrong wars
but every war is
anguish and untimely death
and cripples and smitten souls.

There are wars that break out
in daylight and wars that begin
at night, but every war
is darkness even on sunny days

and even when flares
turn night into day.

Spring has also arrived here
and walking along our street
I heard the song birds and asked,
"Birds, why are you singing, don't
you know it's war?" but they didn't
heed me and kept on singing.

FANTASIES

When he tells us he hears the stars
singing, his pale monk's face, his dark
eyes, we pretend to listen, oh the singing
of stars, the sweetest of the sweet.

If we told him that he himself is a figment
of our imagination and thus all he hears
is unreal, he wouldn't believe us.

Since there's no alternative, we raise
our eyes to the sky, the grayish clouds lumbering
along like a herd of animals on their way
to the lake for their evening drink, and right
above us, the huge boar, new king of the forest,
shakes its snout in a menacing way, its tusks
growing red in the glowing sunset.

THE COASTAL ROAD, BEFORE DAWN

It's still non-light, that same blurriness between
darkness and hazy glow through which the angel
traced the lintels of those ordained to be exterminated,
and already the thunder of heavy trucks rolling in
from unknown zones, loaded with unimaginable
horror, as if arriving from the depths of inferno—

     and then the birds

A MILITARY CORRESPONDENT REMEMBERS

Sent for copy to the Northern Front
I ducked, terrified, behind dark
basalt rocks, and even though
there wasn't any sea, I heard it
crashing against the shores
of my ears, drowning out
those whistles and thuds.

Sent for copy to the Southern Front
I burrowed like a mole deep
into the sand so that not even
a puff of breath would rustle
one golden grain. Above, inhuman
whines of fabricated birds tore
apart the sky's blue *parochet.*

In that war there was no Central Front
but I keep brooding on the central
point to a story about the harsh sound
scrapers make when peeling charred flesh
off the inner seams of a burnt-out tank.

Parochet: Curtain of the Ark.

SILENCE

We grew up on silence. Because of the oath
sworn over the gun, the lone candle flickering

in the dark. Because we were a new generation,
praised for holding back—clenched mouths, emotion

kept under wraps. Reared on lofty sentiments
we created ourselves out of fury, severing

our umbilical cords with our own teeth. I was dry-eyed
when a city boy, my only friend, drowned in the irrigation

pool of the kibbutz; when she whose name is erased
from my memory mocked my ardent, puppy love;

and not one whimper escaped my bitten lips when Yoel,
my high school classmate, the one who gave me his copy

of *The Prisoner of Zenda*, was killed in the naval
commando raid that gold-and-blood summer, the first

of our independence; and no tears when clever Yehiel
left our table on the second floor of the café for good;

and none at the tombstones marking the graves
of my dreams' casualties, overgrown with cacti, fenced

by rusty barbed wire in the cemetery of my life.
We grew up on silence, hard and dark as basalt

and if my eyes seem moist to you today—it's the north
wind scorching them with icy fingers. Indeed, let the wind

be blamed for that sound coming from my direction, that
howling like a wounded beast, tired unto death.

SEQUEL

"The sky is falling! The sky is falling!" squawked
the frantic chicken rushing about the yard as if
possessed. It was so terrified it ignored the fat
earthworms crawling in the dirt after the recent rain.
Naturally, no one heeded the chicken because we all
know that folktale. A little while later the sky did fall.
There were no stars in the black hole that replaced it
Also, there was nobody to look for the stars, nor lament
the fate of the truth-telling chicken.

ECHO

When I was a child, and the world was still bright
and exotic, I contracted diphtheria. Banished
behind shutters I could hear birdsong and children's
chatter floating up from the guava and lemon trees
in our neighbor's courtyard. My mother tried
to hush that unruly chorus as I lay gasping
for breath. Later they told me I nearly died, only
a miracle saved me. Now, so many years later,
I find myself thinking that maybe I really did leave
this earth before tasting of its fruits, especially
the forbidden, and all that has transpired since
never happened and I am merely an echo growing fainter
behind locked shutters among guava and lemon trees
in a courtyard that perhaps did, or did not, exist.

Echo: In Hebrew, both an echo and a divine voice.

LATELY DEAD PEOPLE

Lately dead people stroll about
in my dreams. Sometimes
they are kin and sometimes

I don't know who they are, or
where they come from. They speak
the language of the dead, and grief

washes over me like lunar eddies.
They beg me to do something. Even
if I grasped what they wanted

I couldn't grant their wishes. *Please*,
I say. *Be patient. Maybe in time
I will learn to understand, or at least

read your lips.* But they go on
in their strange tongue until
they fade away, their eyes filled

with loss. When the alarm rings
I'm already up, clinging to my life
as it slips through my fingers.

SIREN

One siren wail opens
Memorial Day and one
ends it. Among my friends
are some war casualties and
some victims of terminal diseases
and all of them left this world
without taking leave
of me and without demanding
to be remembered. Yet I
remember them, each
and every one of them, now
as I sit in my empty home,
my travel knapsack by my side
and they are silently waiting
with me for the third
siren, audible only to us, shrill
and persistent, reverberating
in tunnels of blood.

OASIS

YOU DIDN'T ASK

When I arrived, you didn't ask
for passport, or permit, or
references, though my sun-scorched
cheeks were coarse with stubble,
my fingernails grimy, and my tongue
stumbled over the simplest syllables.

You looked. And then you placed
a cool palm over my burning eyes.
It was still cool later on
when you offered me water, water,
a fistful of dates, and that bountiful
oasis between your thighs.

TOPOGRAPHY

My motherland is
your bodyland:
your breasts—the hills
of Jerusalem,
your belly—the coastal plain,
and between your thighs sometimes
the saltiness of the Dead Sea
and sometimes
the sweet Kinneret.

Kinneret: Hebrew for Lake Tiberias.

FINGERS

When you entwine your fingers
in my fingers our strength doesn't multiply
or grow threefold, it doesn't become stronger
at all, as fables would have us believe.
Nothing happens except warmth flowing
from naked fingers to naked fingers.

And yet
when you entwine your fingers in mine
I know it was worthwhile to take
my old knapsack, pack it with an image
of the motherland and other basic necessities
and set forth, middle-aged and scarred
by my past, towards an uncertain dawn,
with no guarantees, from an airport with signs
reading, "Beware: freshly waxed floor."

DIRECTION

They keep telling me
I've got two left hands
but I say: it's no disaster, the heart
also beats on the left side of the body.

Today I caught sight of myself
in the mirror, the sparse hair
still remaining to me white
as fresh snow before passers-by
crush it underfoot.

How surprised you'll be on your return
when I clasp you to my heart
with my two left hands, the one
refusing to veer rightward.
And I'll ask: *Don't you think*
time has taught me which direction
to follow, and to stick to it?

AT THE ACUPUNCTURIST'S WAITING ROOM

At the acupuncturist's waiting room two cranes
alight on the Chinese fan
on the wall, or perhaps
they are preparing to take off—no way
to tell for sure, nor if
the gentle ringing
of porcelain cups is real
or a figment of my imagination.

Indeed, time is eternal here, sifted
clean of place and past, the gnawing pain
of my missing rib, my homeland.
Opening the I Ching I read:
a group of girls, like a school
of fish, is led to the palace.
There is no sign of disharmony.

TONGUES

King Solomon knew the tongues of man, animal
and bird: he spoke rhino to the rhino and bee-eater
to the bee-eater and to each of his one thousand
wives spoke of his love for her in her own tongue.

But I whisper only to you, in my tongue,
which isn't yours, a few words of little
import, then wrap myself up in silence
and let the birds talk in my stead.

YOUR WINDOW

Your window is a sea
and birdcall and sun
bathing in dew.

Your window is a world
before the Tree of Knowledge
was planted.

Your window is a mouth
caressed by kisses
floating on a mild breeze.

But with neither language
nor words your lips create
sun, sea, the Song of Songs.

INNOCENCE

Hi sun.
Hi feathery clouds.
Hi green leprechaun,
fingers of crocuses.
Hi little Korean barber
trimming my hoary beard with respect.
Hi moment of innocence
when I believed everything was possible.

CITRONELLA

Alone on the wooden deck of your house
I sniff a sprig of citronella and surprisingly
my eyes grow moist: a whippoorwill cries out
in the long summer dusk and its grief sounds
almost human, as if lamenting our recurring
losses in the baseball game of life.

The lovers around us have stopped loving
because routine deadens love, or because
pheromones cease exciting the brain, but I know
here on the wooden deck of your house, sniffing
the citronella sprig, that all I need is
to touch your hand to find a small corner
in this defeated world of ours and sing
of its brief glory in the prolonged summer
dusk, and the whippoorwill, and love.

LACEWORK

You walk alone in the meadow,
a light breeze caressing your face, arms,
and eddies of a kind sun flicker in your hair.

You pluck stems of wild wheat, cattails yellowed
by summer, a lacework of primeval flowers that you
touch to the slightly parted lips of your childhood.

If I called you Eve you wouldn't
know why. This glowing
interlude is innocent of even one
faint heartbeat of foreboding.

DESTROYER IN EDEN

They walk about Eden as if it were their own,
holding hands, naked, innocent
of sex, slums, literary theories.
Trees rustle their boughs for them,
the grasses bow down in the light breeze,
how happy they are without knowing
what happiness is, how proud he is without
knowing pride, describing the kinds
of animals they meet on their way, pausing
to give them names. On the other side
of the island the destroyer is at anchor,
grey, low on the water, more silhouette
than something real, but they don't see it.
It belongs to another era that has not yet
arrived, and only God can foresee in the river
of time with its four headwaters an era
He has dreamed up in order to play
His games of creation and destruction.

BORROWED TIME

Every day I coin a new pet name for you
from the most precious metals, some not yet
excavated from the depths of the earth, to confuse
those who would hasten the final end, but
darling mine, we live on borrowed time.

And when, like ancient Hebrews, we cross
dry land between banks ablaze with crimson
foliage and I refer to occult as well as
familiar sources, you don't really listen
but darling mine, we live on borrowed time.

We return under a frozen moon, neither wiser
nor more foolish, and all around are ruins of lost
empires, scaffolds, monuments promising eternal
life already picked clean by archaeologists,
but darling mine, we live on borrowed time.

We switch on the TV, listen to voicemail,
eat a bit, and retire at lights-out to take our necessary
rest, drained of temptation, and dream about what
we are not and what we shall not be,
but darling mine, we live on borrowed time.

EARTHQUAKE

At the crack of dawn an earthquake
rattled my dream. I stretched out
my hand, then pulled it back bereft
of falling stars and you. Angels
ascend and descend Jacob's ladder
scorning Richter's scale. At the edge
of summer, under dusty ficus trees,
someone was halting upon his thigh
as if the hollow were out of joint
or like a cripple from the next war.

ASTEROID

An asteroid is falling towards earth and will probably hit thirty years from now.
　　　　　　　　　　　The Washington Post

Five stairs above ground level
I occupy a good position
from which to observe the world. The wind
drives the last shriveled leaves
from the trees. The sky is clean
of falling stars. And at a distance
vast enough to stay uninvolved, Beit Jala
shoots at Gilo and Gilo returns fire.

Do we still have enough time
for soul searching? Or have we grown
callous from watching too many
doomsday movies about meteorites
crashing into the earth?

Leaves swirl around my head like a tiara
or a halo and when you come out to the porch
to tell me about Beit Jala and Gilo
trading fire, I, from my vantage point
five stairs above the ground, know
that I'm involved up to my ears
and that the asteroid will hit its objective
if not thirty years hence, then
in its own time and space.

Beit Jala: A Palestinian townlet south of Jerusalem; Gilo: an Israeli suburb of Jerusalem. The two became known for incessant skirmishes during the Second Intifada.

HUSH

From the hideout of your black fur collar you whisper *hush*.
The frosted grass whispers *hush*. The evergreens whisper *hush*.
The squirrel has stopped racing up the tree and whispers *hush*.
Something is going to happen in this horrible, wonderful world,
perhaps now, perhaps later, but I wait.

NOON, ON FAIRFAX ROAD

And if I told you that today, at noon, on Fairfax
Road, walking in this thin drizzle, I saw Death
with a face like mine, not amidst big waves, but
wearing a business suit and a new London Fog,
one hand holding a briefcase and in the other a list
of addresses wrapped in plastic, inspecting the houses
like a real estate agent, would you believe me?
And if I added that he nodded to me and we exchanged
a few pleasantries, would you believe me?
Oh yes, you would.

But if I told you that today, at noon, on Fairfax
Road, the thin drizzle ceased and a blue window
opened up in a leaden sky and through it a young
sun was revealed, all distance erased, hands
clasping hands on a common shore and multitudes
of birds taking off with a magnificent clap of wings,
would you believe me? And if I added that all colors
of the rainbow appeared, promising that no more
floods would visit the earth, would you believe me?
No, you wouldn't.

EXTREMITIES

Here, rocks wrapped in burnt sienna
look like Indians huddling in their blankets
and the sinewy stilts of adobes perch in plots
of hard soil. An arctic chill. Tomorrow
it will snow. Meanwhile the sky's vast plain
catches itself on the ridge's horns, our breath
is short: ravens' caws rip these heights
to shreds. And you, where are you? Soaring
off to different climes, time zones, vistas,
and stars not marked on local charts. My ravenous
hands are empty, and where shall I search
for you in the infinite sea of change, gnawing
at the memory of your walk, voice, flesh? Nothing
to hang on to but the mantra of your name
and face this harsh, primeval landscape
we both shall return to, tripping over glacial
syllables, my angel of light, my black swan.

HOUSES

Like a tired migratory bird you drop
your head on my shoulder and I know
what you want from me: protection
from this bad world.

But I also know that every shelter I built
for you—straw, wood, brick—all
were washed away in the storm.
The only thing left for me to give

is my old, bruised body, swaying
in the slightest puff of wind, but it's all yours,
whether standing upright or collapsing—
come, hide in it.

BY THE RIVERS OF BABYLON

I want to clasp you to my heart
but my arm doesn't move.

I want to tell you words of love
but my lips don't move.

The love in me
has let my right hand forget
its cunning and my tongue cleave
to the roof of my mouth.

What shall I do?

I'll hold you with my left arm
and keep silent until
you hear me.

AT THE END

At the end of the summer solstice days begin
to grow shorter, and this happens in the fullness

of summer, when all the fruits of the garden
ripen, even the forbidden, and their juice

drips in the absence of plucking. And books
of wisdom become wiser and less easy

to interpret, and lost wars become even more lost
in caves of time, and caravans of camels

wander between reason and rashness as if
their drivers forgot where they set out from

and where they are going. At the end of summer
solstice nights begin getting longer and the woman

whose beauty is stamped on my eyes dozes
on the couch facing the flickering screen

while I do my best to live as intimately with pain
as I did with love and passion, and when the doctor

asks me whether I entertain terminal thoughts I
am momentarily embarrassed before categorically

denying it, not to mention the fact that winter solstice
is still far away, and the cold, and the dark.

KNIFE IN THE RIBS

WEB

Is a motherland a shirt you can put on
or take off according to need?

I promise myself not to log on to the web
to find out what's happening in the Land—
in all the languages of the world, nowhere
is "Land" so precise, so significant—I promise
myself, but don't keep my promise. If I can't
keep promises to myself, why do I bother?

And thus I log on, read, gnash my teeth, cry
with dry eyes, pull out hair that I don't have, burn
in the flames of a hell I don't believe in, pick up pieces
of the shattered dream and kiss them like Jeremiah
among the ruins, kissing the bones of his beloved dead.

Tell me, all you pundits, is a motherland
a shirt?

In a famous midrash about the prophet Jeremiah, he wanders among those killed by the Babylonians during the destruction of Jerusalem, picking up bones and kissing them.

LOSS

A man whose son has gone missing
in the forest sits on a tree trunk at the edge
of it. He doesn't know why his son entered
the forest, maybe to hunt, or fish, or collect
rare flowers, or to discover animals not
included in the field guides. The father sits
and waits, maybe his son will emerge
from the thicket of ferns, unsteady
on his feet, eyes dull, clothes torn, wild
beard reaching his breast, but that's
his lost son, how can he desert his post?

I sit at the entrance of the labyrinth
in which my country has vanished.
I don't know why my country is lost
or what I should do to reclaim it
and the sunlight, the good breeze,
the songbirds in groves of oleander
and acacia. For days I've been sitting
here, my eyes dim, cheeks stubbly,
clothes in tatters, shoes patched, the bread
in my knapsack dry and moldy, but this is
my lost country, how can I desert my post?

SIBBOLETH

> *Then they said unto him, Say now Shibboleth: and he said Sibboleth: for he could not frame to pronounce it right. Then they took him, and slew him at the passages of Jordan.*   Judges, ch. 12, v. 6

This morning chipmunks scampered
among pine and birch, racing
to complete their small, crucial
missions before winter clasps
the forest to its icy breast. Suddenly
from out of a thicket straddling
two seasons a streak of vivid blue
rent the air. If it were the Bird
of Happiness it vanished as suddenly
as it appeared. There, trapped between
worlds, I knew even if pursued unto
Jordan's passages and ordered to say
shibboleth, despite having mastered
the correct pronunciation, I'd answer
sibboleth, tongue stubbornly savoring
each syllable, eyes unflinching
from the blade and its dull gleam.

EARTH

This good, fertile earth is not mine, will never
be mine, no matter how graciously it invites me
to rest in peace here, despite my having
nothing left in me to give, nothing whatsoever.

That parched, lean land is mine, with its *khamsins*
coursing through my blood, seeping into the dry
furrows around my mouth, sapping my strength
as I toss feverishly in your alien bed.

Such grief you caused me, saying, "Carpe diem."

Khamsin: Hot wind blowing in from the Sahara desert.

SILENCE OF THE BUILDER

Many days have passed since I ceased
building the tower whose top may reach
unto heaven. The scaffolding still stands
where it used to when work was proceeding
apace, although the onslaught of sun and rain
has wreaked serious damage. Mounds of brick
and mortar rise here and there and the spilled
lime burns like a white fire. Visitors
rarely come. When they do, they ask questions
I can't answer. Not because I don't know
the appropriate reply, but because I've been out
of practice so long my tongue has become
clumsy. Often I can't comprehend the dialect
or accent. Last night a thunderstorm rattled
the windows of my shack. It seemed as though
the lightning signaled to me in a new code.
I had no desire to crack it. You approached
and took my hand. I saw the pulse in your throat
failed to beat with its old intensity. Water
in my mouth tasted bitter, like hemlock. The plain
of our silence stretches beyond the horizon.

CASSANDRAS

Making love we turn our backs on the dawn
of crows, black robed Cassandras

whose warnings go unheeded, the cities tossing
in their beds with dirty thoughts and polluted lungs,

our previous life. The miracle hasn't occurred
and even if we guessed right, it still wouldn't—

disappointment whets our pleasure. We are no longer
young and therefore we insist on the correct proportion

of tenderness and violent sensuality. How strange
then, when later we go down to the kitchen

for coffee, we wait for the whistling kettle
as if it were the Doomsday siren.

MEGIDDO

The clock's pendulum at your house moves
with an aesthetic lack of sound once to the right,
once to the left, and man's days and nights run out
silently, once to the right, once to the left.

In the burnt-out bus among scorched
body parts, two corpses embrace
and it seems the lovers clutched
during their last spark of consciousness,
their hearts exploding simultaneously,
indivisible, to the right, or to the left.

At your house man's days and nights run out
with an aesthetic lack of sound to the subtle
movements of a pendulum swinging indifferently
in opposite directions, but at the Megiddo juncture
in a horrifying clap of thunder, life and death are as one
annihilating love along with any aesthetic judgment.

Megiddo: A kibbutz in Israel close to where a Palestinian suicide bomber blew up a bus; also the Hebrew name for Armageddon.

CAGE

In the body's cage the canary soul
struggles, hurling itself against

the narrow bars, rusty but strong enough
to prevent it from breaking out.

Liberation, freedom, space—these
concepts cause its heart to go wild

and the bird begins to sing to the sky
visible through parted curtains, a wondrous

feat because it is so far away. My innocent
canary soul, protected by the cage of my body, you

sing to impossible hope, unaware of the solitary
hawk circling in the same, distant sky.

FALL

The foreign air is more tender now.
A telephone call is a way of traveling

to a place where there is no guarantee
of return. I know these leaves, bright

and changing, will drop off and branches
will be left stark naked. The runners

race by, lungs bursting, keeping nothing
in reserve for the End of Days. At night

I clutch the edge of the bed so I don't fall out
of my membership in the community of man.

NANTUCKET

"If I draw the world's sorrow in a straight line from here
eastward, I'll arrive in Portugal," said the dreaming woman.

The moons of her eyes blanched in the fog and at the foot
of the bluff, the ocean's surf crashed against the shore like cries

of drowning mariners. "Don't call me Ishmael and Queequeg's
coffin won't be there for my last travail," I said. "And if

I draw my own sorrow in a straight line from the top of the cliff
through the heather thicket and over the deep, it would touch

the lost planet of my dreams." But the faceless woman
ignored me, shaking off drops of water from her hair, wrapping

herself in fog as in a bridal veil. She extinguished the moons
of her eyes and instead switched on two rusty oranges.

WINDFALL

In the Caribbean, tens of people die each year from falling coconuts.

The world is a gaping mouth of an idiot: a man
stands under a coconut tree, waiting for the ripe,
rough-skinned fruit to drop and crack open
his head with one fell swoop. He does not move,
his eyes closed, a shudder running through
his listening flesh, but the fruit takes its time
and the world is a gaping mouth of an idiot
not knowing what the man expects, and when.

INSOMNIA

That night, sleep deserted the king, and he ordered the book of records, the annals, to be brought; and it was read to the king.
                                                    Esther, ch. 6, v. 1

I've got insomnia, but no one
to read me memoirs or histories

of good deeds done for me by my friends
or bad things done to me by my enemies, both

beneficial for renewing slumber
and dreams of gratitude or vengeance.

Tel Aviv recedes in the impartial haze
of time, my beloved's face becomes

unfamiliar to me even in the few obligatory
photos. Only speculations about the origin

of my accent take on wilder hues, as if
merchants of rare animals for a traveling

circus had trapped me in a cage to entertain
the masses, or scare them to death.

I DREAMED OF A GENERAL

"I heard her tears..."
                    Dante Gabriel Rosetti

I dreamed of a triumphant general
and of those who conspired to kill him
and may even have done so. Once
you interpreted my dreams. Now
you shrug. Is the dream too
complicated? Or perhaps you understood
its meaning and refused to tell me?
Tonight, it seems to me, you
cried. I heard your tears.

HEAVINESS

After a sleepless night my eyelids
are heavy as lead ingots:
a worn out image, I know,
but that's how I feel. Everything
is heavy on me, and in me, my country
is heavy and my misfortune
is heavy and my hate
for you is heavy as a noon
siesta taken under a tattered canopy
by workmen hired to excavate
the relics of my life.

FALL BACK

And again time retreats without a battle,
not even a faint protest, its brow crowned
with a garland of withered leaves, oak
and poplar, definitely unromantic,
and whirls of polluted urban smoke.

Let's admit it, we've lost another round,
my fading love, and at the street corner
death awaits us, smiling pleasantly
like an old friend, decked out in a fancy
fur coat, unhurried, unstressed, and from time
to time glancing apologetically
at the elegant watch on his wrist.

IF IT WERE FALL

If it were fall I'd rake
your memory, motherland, like
a pile of wilted leaves, set them ablaze
and when the blue smoke spirals up,
watch it ascend, my eyes stinging.

But now it's winter, the trees
shiver and cold grips the earth
in a vise so tight its bones creak.

And the knife of your memory
lodges in my ribs, burning.

HOLY CITY

You squat on me like a holy
city, every site marked
in the tourist guide.
But in the distance
I can already see the reddening hills
and the insurgents' banners. When
the beacon signals I'll drag upstairs
the barrels of gunpowder, so long hoarded
in the heart's vault, switch on the timer
and when the ticking stops, the spiraling
fire, a burst of thunder, and the final
glorious mushroom.

I RAN

> *Man, why did you run away?*
> Jerzy Andrzievsky, "The Diamond and the Ashes"

I ran because what I craved proved to be
a mirage, I ran because in the wilderness
my body burst into flames, I ran because
when the last *wadi* flooded, my soul
also was washed away, I ran because I'm human
and was afraid the bullet would hit my back
but instead it struck the bull's eye of my heart.

ABRAHAM

When I fell against a stack of idols in my father's store
shattering them, news of the accident flew throughout
Ur of the Chaldees. Gossiping neighbors, ambitious
PR men and subversive elements made a mountain
out of a molehill, an event of profound significance.
And that was the beginning.

Since then He won't loosen his grip, forcing me to wander
from my motherland, its rivers, to a primitive, dry land
and when longing overtook me He pierced
my head, my heart, my soul, my manhood.
He changed my name and harassed me day and night
with whirling visions: *Father of many nations...chosen
people...a promised land...*inflicting His covenant upon me.
He allotted me only a few years to rejoice
in my firstborn, begotten when I was already bent
with age. He prompted my bitter, barren shrew of a wife
to demand that I cast out both boy and mother to an almost
certain desert death. Then, before all nomad tribes,
He made me the fool by granting us an heir long after
we were spent. I was flush with joy, but soon He was at it
again, designing cruel games to test my faith: I must give
up my son, my only son, the one I love, for a burnt offering.

Now we are climbing the mountain, my son and I,
under a vast expanse of sky, the hot, bald Negev
on every side. The two servants and the ass remain
at the foot of the mountain, leaving the boy to carry
the wood. He knows nothing, nor does his mother—
else she would have taken her life. I am silent. Only
the cold blade freezes my flesh, only the glittering
white blossoms of the broom bush glimpsed

through half-closed eyes. Why didn't I refuse?
I could have cast off His yoke from my
century-old neck, rejected a harsh One in favor
of a bickering family of gods, all of them lusting
for power, easy to play one against the other.
Now I choke on His demand for my poor man's ewe…

A step. Another step. The mountain peak
looms, the sun's burning rays beat down
on our heads, no movement, no sound, no flash
of a ram's horn, no hawk's fluttering wing.
Should anything happen when we arrive, no matter
what, nothing will change the wilderness
that once was my heart.

CALENDAR

All I'm left with from my country is a calendar
hanging in the kitchen, decorated with photographs

of landscapes already appearing unfamiliar, as if
they were views of a planet first seen

by an astronaut. I observe these landscapes
longingly, studying them like a student

before an exam, and when you are absent
from my side, I press them close to my face,

trying to warm their professional chill, to breathe
life into them in a way that would at least

foster the illusion that we had never parted.

COFFEE THOUGHTS

To cut a poem short.
To lengthen a life.

THE HEART'S FIELD OF STUBBLE

VAGARIES OF TIME

Hour clutches hour like Jacob
his brother's heel, not because he
wanted to emerge first from the womb
but to elude slipping into the void.

Do you remember how I leaped after you
climbing that hill near Arad, our laughs
entwining, my legs shedding their years
as they strained up the warm stones, and how
I was the first to reach the top, how I loved
you then, no need to exchange language
for language, trusting Time's sympathy,
the simple passion of our bodies?

Old fool, she was only a sleight of hand
kept in play by a dexterous juggler: now
put a stone under your head in the wilderness
of a cold city, wrap yourself up in a blanket
of stars, mutter incantations in an ancient tongue
as you feel how distance closes in on you
like a bounty hunter of souls, and soon
the blanket will be yanked off your shivering
body, and a hostile voice will demand
your documents and inform you they have
expired, that your time has come to stand trial.

IN PRAISE OF HATE

My friend, a clever woman, tells me hate
is the most democratic emotion. Mulling
it over, I decide she's hit the nail on the head
and by that measure, I am a democrat par excellence.
Oh, without reservation, with no shred
of bias, I hate those who spill innocent blood,
no matter what race or religion, those who grind
the faces of the poor, suck their marrow, those
who amass fortunes, speculate in misery, masters
of corruption, rabbis of coercion, parasites
of sanctity, feeding on the dead, sowing strife
to promote themselves, ravenous for power, rolling
sanctimonious eyes, spreading cheap promises,
priests of deceit, swindlers, directors of obscenity,
scribes of rot, those who sell their own birthright
for a mess of lentils or any other bean, offspring
of Satan concealing their horns and hooves, spinners
of false dreams, worshippers of abstraction decked out
in their finery of high art or tawdry clichés, see how
they parade, frothing at the mouth, stoking the hysteria
of the mob, and of course I hate you, apple of my eye,
you who swore to love me forever, yea verily I hate
the whole lot, no one shall escape unpunished. Selah.

IN MY DREAM MY LIFE

In my dream my life was a stretch of deserted
railroad tracks, grass growing between the crossties,
tracks rusty because of the weather.

And in my dream I walked along those tracks
and after awhile I stopped and sat down
and buried my face in my arms.

IT'S EASIER TO LAMENT

It's easier to lament the sinking of the State
than that face reflected in the mirror.
To the telephone call from afar, how are you,
your health, I respond by expressing shock
at what has been happening there, in that place,
not at my own decaying flesh, the bags
under my eyes puffy as empty promises.

But when evening falls during the foreign
summer solstice, and after a thunderstorm
when the hot season has not yet regained
its prowess, air shimmers and a double rainbow
appears, one glowing with bright colors
the other faded, washed out in the pale azure.

In this unholy land, does meteorology
change into theology? Is this the sign
meant to remind us that the old story
from Genesis is still true, and then some,
and its message doesn't grow stale, but
is renewed all over the globe?

And then, while still musing, the individual
and collective amalgamate seize the ancient
promise that only yesterday seemed so
ridiculously stupid. The heavenly phoenix
burns to ashes and again grows wings.

COMING BACK

This time on my return, Ephraim will not
be at the airport to pick me up, nor will
Azriel cross the Yarkon Bridge
to see me again.

But they will be there
when I join them, and I know for sure
they are keeping a seat for me.

And because they know I hate
fish, they will invite me to settle down
at a table heaped with the Middle Eastern
dishes I love so much and wait patiently
for the arrival of coffee and good talk.

MOTHERLAND

This soft pearly light,
grayish, pre-dawn,
settling so tenderly
on your rooftops, the solar boilers,
the TV antennas, on
you, Tel Aviv.

DISTANCE

I stretch my arm
and strain and strain
but cannot touch you.
You are so far away.

Yet I ask for the impossible:
that you touch me even if
every flight-stretched vein bursts open,
that you hear my heart through
the din of the world.

Perhaps war will break out tomorrow.
When you come home from work tonight
I want you to see my dark eyes
etched on your window-pane.

TIMES

In summer, the hot, humid days
dawn with the time of cooing doves
followed by the time of cawing crows
succeeded by the time of birds singing
a thousand notes and trills
I find impossible to describe.

Also, I cannot explain how returning
from you to my country, I begin the time
of waiting, turning into the time of searing
pain, succeeded by the time of rage
and gnashing of teeth, followed
by the time of dull grief.

And then the time of the body politic, time
of the bleeding horizon beyond marinas
where luxury yachts bob on the water, the envy
of passersby swept away by street cleaners.

But the ancient earth, still there beneath
asphalt parking lots, goes on, concealing
the primeval chaos deep below, counting
the days until the time of bursting forth arrives.

NINTH MONTH

In September, in the impossible land, light
changes, the breeze grows refined in the uppermost
branches of the eucalyptus, and the sea, an enormous
music box, croons love songs, all of them
pianissimo. And on the moon Buddha's rabbit
again concocts the elixir of life.

LONG DISTANCE

Talking with you you're still
in one day and I in the next
yet the words between us
are so close, as if my lips
were grazing the rose
of your ear.

They know: the speed of light,
the rules of natural law,
but I, old fool that I am,
insist: it's love.

AND THEY MERIT GLORY
For Jesse, researcher of songbirds, who told me

Why do You curse us now? Today mad John's four horsemen
sweep across the sky—cranes, swallows, storks, wild geese—all
the migratory birds spreading contagion while we are the ones
taking flight from the cold, the dark. Even the robin
redbreast flashing its fiery passion with pride
leaves West Nile fever in its wake. But the finches
go on singing the incorruptible light, neither cage, nor
isolation, nor silence deters them, their tiny hearts
beating like bells, they sing and sing with every ounce
of their being, singing the promise and the hope
and the world rests on them, and they merit glory.

POEMS FROM THE RENTED HOUSE

Doubt

You told me in the beginning you didn't love me,
that it took time. I loved you from the first, wholly,
without reservation, paying no heed to the cost
and now, arriving at the house we rented
for the summer, we stroll down to the river
and find signs warning us against the poison ivy.

July

Cooler today. Grey skies. The beech sentinels
grow dark at their posts. A squirrel hunches over
the banister's wooden pineal, a Roman senator
brooding on the Empire's decline, or Yoda
of Star Wars, debating the best way
to train a young Jedi for future
intergalactic missions.

Instinctively, I take your palm in mine, letting
my warmth flow through your fingers. That's all
I can offer—no victory, no dominion, no
light saber, no cliché, like *sic transit
gloria mundi*, as a mild summer rain obscures
the view from the French window.

After You Drove Away

You drove away from the rented house
on unfamiliar roads toward undefined goals
and the angels of anxiety my heart
dispatched in the drizzle to hover
over your head lost their way before
you sensed their presence. Who, then
shall I appoint to watch over you
in this world so at odds with itself?
All of Argus's one hundred eyes are shut,
a faint smile fluttering over his lips: he dreams
of one day, one night, when he will be
relieved from standing guard.

And what if you stray to the dirt trail
winding through the mighty oaks where Hansel's
and Gretel's witch hunts in the forest for fresh
human prey to bake in her oven?

There are graver worries, say the experts, shrugging
off my despair; but the twenty years of my love
wring their hands and rush pale-faced to read
the crime reports in the local paper.

Venison

Tonight they will eat venison. Earlier, he spoke
harshly against hunting deer. Later, he stopped
abruptly, as if an apple were stuck

in his mouth, and mulled over the condiments
to serve with the steak.

In the morning the river flowing through the thick
trees is dark green. It's easy to explain: shadows
of foliage on the water. But to sit
on the bench the owners set on the bank
and gaze at the fleeting current is to know
change is constant.

His beloved refills the bird feeder each day. The house
is rented, but she follows the instructions as if
she had written them herself. He sticks to the role
of amateur ornithologist, identifying the beneficiaries
of her largesse: blue jay, raven, finch, sparrow, warbler,
cardinal. Therefore, the Saint of Birds will forgive
her trespasses, but she will never pardon him
for the least grain of his love.

At Dawn

At dawn the fog is so thick that shapes
are fuzzy: trees, people, birds, squirrels. Even
a motherland is suddenly abstract. Maybe
it's to be found only in travelogues of ancient
explorers or in fairy tales. No option but to wait,
not impatiently, for the clearing that has been
forecast, which may reaffirm a word that now
has lost meaning, or might still be valid.

Art

> *Ceci n'est pas une pipe.*
> Magritte

A pipe isn't a pipe,
a meadow isn't a meadow,
a fir isn't a fir,
Moshe isn't Moshe;
but you are—you,
and thanks to you, thanks to the light
touch of that little finger of yours
a pipe becomes a pipe,
a meadow becomes a meadow,
a fir becomes a fir,
Moshe becomes Moshe,
and life becomes worthwhile
again.

Idle Days

Oh, idle days....
The feathery clouds do not stir in the blue,
not even a tiny breeze flutters the poplar leaves.
The song birds, too, have fallen silent in the noonday
heat and the world's grief is buried deep in the earth
and the diggers doze in the shade, their
pickaxes and shovels idle by their side.

Only One Day More

This morning, before setting off for massage
and pool, you picked up a dry leaf felled
by a whimsical breeze and presented it to me
with the gloomy face of a child. And it was
strange, since the summer was still going
strong, but I didn't want to interpret anything
in the light of mere symbol.

Inconsolable, you drove off on your errands
and for a long time I observed the dry meadow
through the screen door (the air conditioner
pleasantly humming). In a short while we'll
set forth to the airport. Is a man more
absent from his life at a rented house
than in his own home?

Coda

Farewell green land,
farewell water. Farewell
sweet, dreamless sleep, no
fire, no history, no Jerusalem.

DO YOU REMEMBER

A spring of ashy sky and a timid
drizzle timid rain scattering diamonds
over the young pines, erect
and monkish like God's candles.

Or the sunny days at Rakefet
in the Galilee, the prophetic golden fire
in rocks, terebinths, bees and thorns,
our bodies' pure passion, the sudden
moment when you no longer
said **"your"** country?

DIVISIONS

This morning the train crossed the Continental Divide.
From here on the division is clear: On this side all rivers
flow eastward, on the other, westward. Over the long
years of our love we have been rushing in our own
direction, you westward, I eastward, twisting and
turning to pour ourselves into each other. Still, in dreams
and poems that stream from that source we merge
into one steadfast river, its mighty waters coursing
through a persistent channel until emptying into the last sea.

JUST IN SPITE

A cold, grey, low, fist-clenched morning:
winter on the East coast, no surprises.
And I, just in spite, suddenly desire
a poppy for my heart's button hole. Why
this odd sense of celebration? wondered
the solemn crow in his dark business suit.
I couldn't enlighten him and also, there were no
poppies to be had in this season. So I pluck
a flushed twig of heavenly bamboo and go forth
into the world with an unbuttoned breast.

JOY

So many books are scattered on the floor
of my room. Some I read from beginning
to end, others, only half-way
because they are too beautiful
to end. And some I haven't read
at all because I lack the prerequisite
courage or despair.

Time will go by according to its custom.
Already I won't be there when one day
a boy with not a drop of my blood
in his veins will enter my room, idly
pick up a book from the floor. He'll open it

at random and read a few lines.
His voice will be loud and clear.

He'll read only a few lines
but what joy will fill the room
that once was my own!

AROMA

There's nothing I like better
than morning coffee
and my love for you is the aroma
of the rest of my life.
So, love of mine, let's
sip morning coffee,
together.

REQUEST

And what would you like for yourself?
Only this:
a slab of stone, smooth-edged,
from the quarry overlooking
the sea, a safe shelter even
on stormy nights, cool
during the long sunny days,
a secret Israel inside,
scent of acacia in its sinews
and the sweetness of figs.

About the Author

MOSHE DOR, born in Tel Aviv in 1932, is a major figure in contemporary Israeli literature. Author of some 40 books of poetry, interviews and children's verse, his most recent book in English translation is *Khamsin: Memoirs and Poetry of a Native Israeli*. As a young man, Dor joined the Hagana and later served as a military correspondent in the Israeli Army until completing his reserve service. For many years he was on the editorial board of *Ma'ariv,* one of  Israel's leading newspapers. Dor is the recipient of the Bialik Prize, Israel's top literary award, and twice winner of Israel's Prime Minister's Award in Literature. He has served as president of Israel's P.E.N. Center; Israel's Counselor for Cultural Affairs in London, and Distinguished Writer-in-Residence at the American University, Washington, D.C.

Dor's work has been translated into more than 20 languages, including Arabic, Chinese and Dutch. Dor himself is a prolific translator of American poets into Hebrew, publishing volumes by Robert Bly, Rita Dove, Robert Hass, William Matthews, Naomi Shihab Nye, Charles Simic, and James Wright, among others. Dor is also well-known for writing the lyrics of *erev shel shoshanim (Evening of Roses)*, one of Israel's most beloved songs, performed worldwide as a wedding song. It has been recorded internationally by artists from Harry Belafonte to Nana Mouskouri.

About the Translator

BARBARA GOLDBERG, raised in Forest Hills, New York, is the author of four books of poetry: *The Royal Baker's Daughter* (2008 Felix Pollak Poetry Prize), *Marvelous Pursuits* (Violet Reed Haas Prize), *Cautionary Tales* (Camden Poetry Award) and *Berta Broadfoot and Pepin the Short* (collaboration with wood engraver Rosemary Covey). Her work has appeared in the *American Poetry Review, Gettysburg Review, Poetry, The Paris Review* as well as in *The Best American Poetry*. Among her awards are two fellowships from the National Endowment for the Arts; numerous grants from the Maryland State Arts Council; the Armand G. Erpf Award from the Translation Center, Columbia University; as well as national awards in fiction, feature writing and speechwriting. A former senior speechwriter for AARP, she is currently visiting writer in the MFA program at American University. She lives in Chevy Chase, Maryland.

Books translated and edited by Moshe Dor and Barbara Goldberg include three anthologies of contemporary Israeli poetry: *Israeli Love Poems, After the First Rain: Israeli Poems on War and Peace* (foreword by Prime Minister Shimon Peres), and *The Stones Remember: Native Israeli Poetry,* (recipient of the Witter Bynner Foundation Award). In addition, they translated and edited *The Fire Stays in Red: Poems by Ronny Someck.*

About The Word Works

THE WORD WORKS, a nonprofit literary organization, publishes contemporary poetry collections and presents public programs. Since 1981, the organization has sponsored the Washington Prize, a monetary award to and book publication for an American or Canadian poet. Monthly, The Word Works offers free literary programs in the Chevy Chase, MD, Café Muse series, and each summer, it holds free poetry programs in Washington, DC's Rock Creek Park. Annually in June, two high school students debut in the Joaquin Miller Series as winners of the Jacklyn Potter Young Poets Competition. Other programs have included workshops, master classes, symposia, international artist retreats, panel discussions, and archival projects with prominent American poets.

As a 501(c)3 organization, The Word Works has received awards from the National Endowment for the Arts, National Endowment for the Humanities, DC Commission on the Arts & Humanities, Witter Bynner Foundation, Poets & Writers, The Writer's Center, Bell Atlantic, the David G. Taft Foundation, and others, including many generous private patrons. The Word Works has established an archive of artistic and administrative materials in the Washington Writing Archive housed in the George Washington University Gelman Library. The Word Works is a member of the Council of Literary Magazines and Presses and distributed by Small Press Distribution.

More information at wordworksbooks.org

Word Works Books

INTERNATIONAL EDITIONS

Yoko Danno & James C. Hopkins, *The Blue Door*
Moshe Dor, *Scorched by the Sun.* Translated by Barbara Goldberg
Moshe Dor, Barbara Goldberg, Giora Leshem, eds., *The Stones Remember*
Myong-Hee Kim, *Crow's Eye View: The Infamy of Lee Sang, Korean Poet*
Vladimir Levchev, *Black Book of the Endangered Species*

WASHINGTON PRIZE BOOKS

Nathalie F. Anderson, *Following Fred Astaire*, 1998
Michael Atkinson, *One Hundred Children Waiting for a Train*, 2001
Carrie Bennett, *biography of water*, 2004
Peter Blair, *Last Heat*, 1999
Richard Carr, *Ace*, 2008
Ann Rae Jonas, *A Diamond Is Hard but Not Tough*, 1997
Frannie Lindsay, *Mayweed*, 2009
Richard Lyons, *Fleur Carnivore*, 2005
Fred Marchant, *Tipping Point*, 1993, 3rd printing 1999
Ron Mohring, *Survivable World*, 2003
Brad Richard, *Motion Studies*, 2010
Jay Rogoff, *The Cutoff*, 1994
Prartho Sereno, *Call from Paris*, 2007
Enid Shomer, *Stalking the Florida Panther*, 1987, 2nd edition 1993
John Surowiecki, *The Hat City after Men Stopped Wearing Hats*, 2006
Miles Waggener, *Phoenix Suites*, 2002
Mike White, *How to Make a Bird with Two Hands*, 2011
Nancy White, *Sun, Moon, Salt*, 1992, 2nd edition 2010

More Word Works Books

THE HILARY THAM CAPITAL COLLECTION

Mel Belin, *Flesh That Was Chrysalis*, 1999
Doris Brody, *Judging the Distance*, 2001
Sarah Browning, *Whiskey in the Garden of Eden*, 2007, 2nd printing 2011
Grace Cavalieri, *Pinecrest Rest Haven*, 1998
Christopher Conlon, *Gilbert and Garbo in Love*, 2003
    Mary Falls: Requiem for Mrs. Surratt, 2007
Donna Denizé, *Broken Like Job*, 2005
W. Perry Epes, *Nothing Happened*, 2010
James Hopkins, *Eight Pale Women*, 2003
Brandon Johnson, *Love's Skin*, 2006
Marilyn McCabe, *Perpetual Motion*, 2012
Judith McCombs, *The Habit of Fire*, 2005
James McEwen, *Snake Country*, 1990
Miles David Moore, *The Bears of Paris*, 1995
    Rollercoaster, 2004
Kathi Morrison-Taylor, *By the Nest*, 2009
Michael Schaffner, *The Good Opinion of Squirrels*, 1996
Maria Terrone, *The Bodies We Were Loaned*, 2002
Hilary Tham, *Bad Names for Women*, 1989
    Counting, 2000
Barbara Ungar, *Charlotte Brontë, You Ruined My Life*, 2011
Jonathan Vaile, *Blue Cowboy*, 2005
Rosemary Winslow, *Green Bodies*, 2007
Michele Wolf, *Immersion*, 2011

ADDITIONAL TITLES

Karren L. Alenier, *Wandering on the Outside*
Karren L. Alenier, Hilary Tham, Miles David Moore, eds., *Winners: A Retrospective of the Washington Prize*
Christopher Bursk, *Cool Fire*
Barbara Goldberg, *Berta Broadfoot and Pepin the Short*
Jacklyn Potter, Dwaine Rieves, Gary Stein, eds., *Cabin Fever: Poets at Joaquin Miller's Cabin*
Robert Sargent, *Aspects of a Southern Story*
    A Woman from Memphis